Contents

Clean Those Clothes!

Hello!
Hi, Alfred!
THROW!
Throw them in!
THROW!

Clothes!
Soap!
CLOSE
PRESS
START
MMMMMMM
Hi, Alfred!

Can you clean these capes?
Okay!
ZIP!
Do you all have capes?
Yes!
Loads of capes!

Hope You Like Pink!

Pink?
Oh, Alfred! Too much soap again!
Who can fight crime looking like this?
Well, I like pink!
JUMP!
TWIST!

Which Clothes?

Which set of clothes goes with which person?

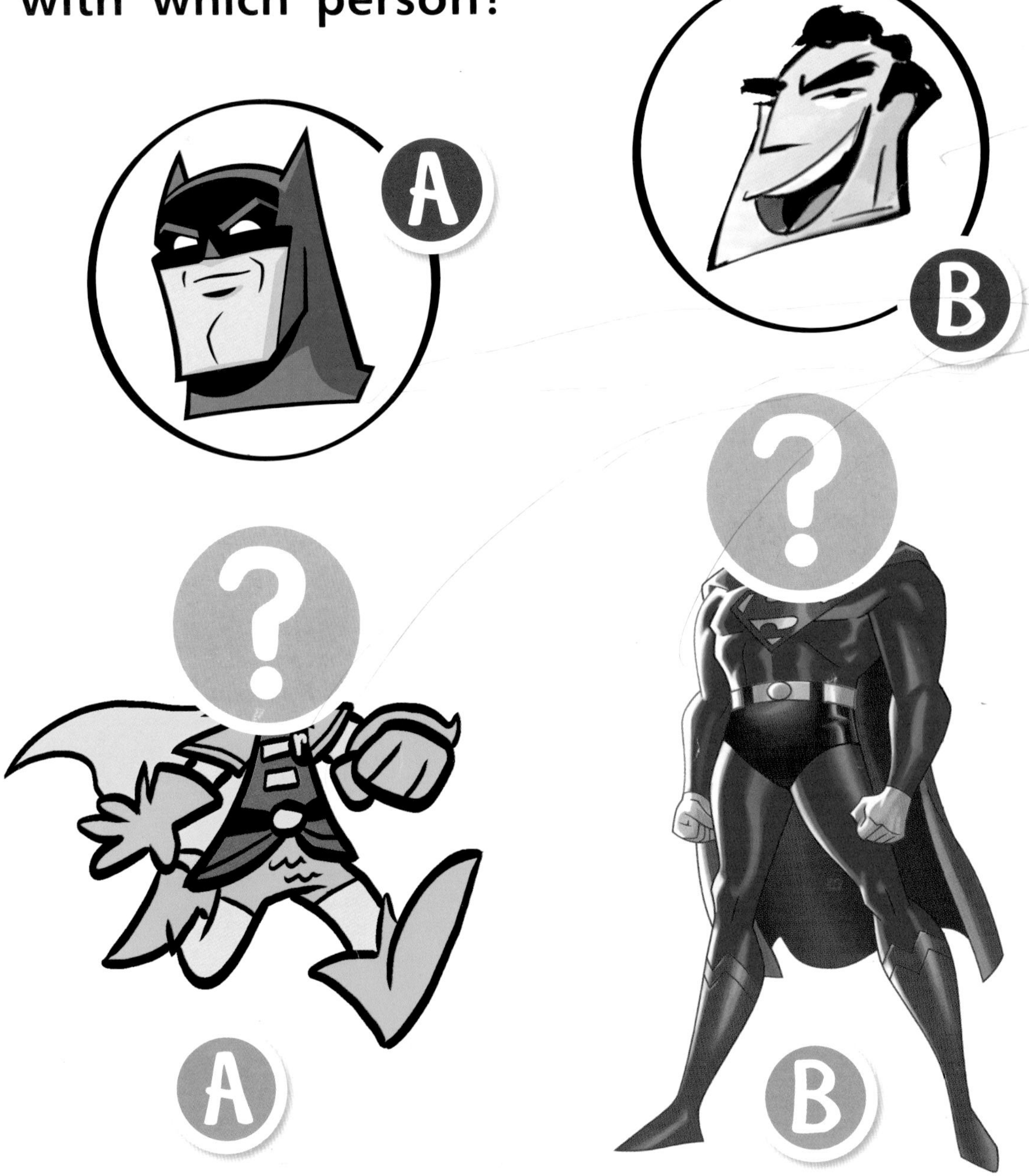

Go to the back to see if you are right!

The Pink Blur!
Sis! You are on telly!
Who? Me?
The Pink Blur saved a helicopter from crashing!
That was you!
How brave!
DAILY PLANET

Er ... do they think that was me?
Yes!
No!
Who was it, then?
Oh no!
Hey!
On telly, they think I am **you**!
Oops ...
It must be those pink clothes!

Well, I suppose I must ...
... get some different clothes on!
Not so pink now!
Hey! He copied **my** clothes!
ZIP!

Pink All Over

You fit right in now!
No!
Too much pink!
Hi, Robin!
Get me out!
But pink is cool!
I am going to stay!
I am not. I am off!

Pink Is Over!
WHOOSH!
Time for some fresh clothes!
WOOF WOOF
ARF ARF
NIGHTWING
Pink again?
No way!
SNIFF
SNIFF
Get the paint!

THROW!
SQUEEZE!
SQUEEZE!
SQUEEZE!
PAINT!
MMMMM!
SHWO, SHWO, SHWO!
Look!
Hey ... cool!
Yes – rainbow! Well, it is better than pink!